Indonesian

Indonesian

Mae Chandra

Published in 2014 by
New Holland Publishers
London • Sydney • Cape Town • Auckland

The Chandlery Unit 114 50 Westminster Bridge Road London SE1 7QY UK
1/66 Gibbes Street Chatswood NSW 2067 Australia
Wembley Square First Floor Solan Road Gardens Cape Town 8001 South Africa
218 Lake Road Northcote Auckland New Zealand

A catalogue record of this book is available at the British Library and
the National Library of Australia.

ISBN: 9781742575520
Managing Director: Fiona Schultz
Design: Linda Gregor
Editor: Simona Hill
Production Director: Olga Dementiev
Printer: Toppan Leefung Printing Ltd (China)

10 9 8 7 6 5 4 3 2 1

Follow New Holland Publishers on
Facebook: www.facebook.com/NewHollandPublishers

Contents

Indonesian
Delicious and exciting

Introduction

The Land and Its People

PREPARE FOR EXCITEMENT

On the beaches of Indonesia, before the sun has risen, bare-chested, bare-footed fishermen still wear the coolie-style hats that protected them from the previous day's piercing sun. After an intense night's labour at sea, they closely examine their catches.

In the dark of the early morning, they quickly sort through their nets to ascertain which fish are suitable for markets, and to calculate how much they will earn from their catch. Indonesia is one of the world's poorest countries but has one of the richest cuisines and an abundance of natural resources. These resources include spices, rice (the staple), coffee, sugar, tobacco, teak, sandalwood, copper and bronze.

There are many such gatherings of fisher-folk who could be members of the Muslim, Buddhist, Hindu, Christian or animist faiths. The fishermen of Indonesia represent an unprecedented 336 ethnic groups in a nation freed from colonialism since 1947 and dictatorship since 1999. Their skin colours vary from jet black to pale brown. An astounding 500 languages and dialects are spoken but bahasa Indonesia, the national language, is taught in Indonesian schools. About 70 per cent of Indonesian people are fluent in this language.

Indonesia's fishermen, including those based on fragile wooden rigs on atolls or anchored at sea for weeks or months on end, have 200 million people to feed. Indonesia land mass is about eight times bigger than the United Kingdom and the fishing grounds in surrounding seas are estimated to be four times larger again.

Indonesia is the world's largest archipelago. It extends for about 5 600 km from the Indian Ocean into the Pacific. There are more than 13 600 separate islands. Most are emerald-green with tropical rainforests or rice paddies amid volcanic eruptions; a few are bare deserts.

Indonesia has been influenced by the cultures of China, India, Arabia, Portugal, Spain,

England, America and the Netherlands. People from these countries mostly arrived in the form of explorer–traders in quest of spices. During World War II, the Japanese also occupied Indonesia for a time; several Japanese culinary influences still linger.

The Dutch dominated Indonesia for 350 years from the 17th century, so a fascinating amalgam of cuisines emerged. The Dutch, bland cuisine was much the richer after integrating with Indonesa the most bountiful, most beautiful, budget beach tourist destination any hedonist could want. So, Indonesian cuisine burst into the most adventurous kitchens on the planet. It was chilli-hot, spicy with cool contrasts, festive, fun to prepare and fabulous to eat.

Sumatra, Java, Bali, Irian Jaya, Kalimantan, Sulawesi and Maluku along with their islands and those of Nusa Tenggara, have diverse ethnic and culinary traditions. In this book we have gathered together dishes from all over Indonesia to give you a taste of the wonderful and varied cuisine of Indonesia.

DAY BY DAY

Each Indonesian family endeavours to eat at least three plates of rice each day; note plates, not bowls. If plates are not available or affordable, disposable banana leaves are used. The implements are fingers (of the clean right hand). Chopsticks are never used with traditional cuisine, though Indonesians may eat with a spoon and fork.

There is little difference between breakfast, lunch and dinner in Indonesia. It is all a question of availability and affordability, so the food may be the same but in varying quantities; always served with rice. Meat, fish and vegetables will be served in fast succession, not together in Chinese-style. Indonesians produce the most tempting and fantastic buffet dinners after sunset. Like Chinese meals, the ingredients in an Indonesian buffet are composed of contrasting dishes; hot and spicy versus mild; sweet versus sour; fried food balanced by superlative steamed dishes.

As is the custom in many Asian countries, it is polite in Java and Bali for guests to leave left-over grains of rice to indicate their gratitude and satiation to the hosts. The hostess, often the cook, may well appreciate left-over rice as it could be used the next day in what is regarded as Indonesia's national dish, nasi goreng (fried rice).

With its religious diversity, Indonesia's festivals are many. Prominent feasts are held mid-year to celebrate harvest, not with rice but, (especially in Bali and Sulawesi) with pig and /or buffalo meat barbecued on bamboo tubes. (Muslims do not eat pork.) The meat is accompanied by copious amounts of white or red tuak, a cloudy sweet-sour palm juice wine.

Non-Muslims like an evening tipple or three of home-brewed tuak, which men imbibe while smoking clove-scented cigarettes. In Bali, beware; their glutinous rice wine (pink and drunk with coconut juice) and rice brandy are potent and potentially dangerous. It's best to stick with local or imported beer or warm or cold tea. The Dutch introduced good coffee-making techniques in the late 1600s and Indonesians have added their own stamp with ground peanuts. If this sounds good, try it out!

Daily Food in Indonesia

SILAKAN MAKAN, SILAKAN MINUM

These words are encouragements to 'Please eat, please drink,' to be uttered when your guests sit at the table to partake of your own, home-cooked Indonesian feast. It may be a rijstafel, in which case you will have just placed a huge bowl of yellow festive rice on the centre of the table and will be ready to surround it with at least as many extra separate dishes as there are guests. One doesn't prepare rijstafel for a romantic tête-a-tête. My first experience of rijstafel was when I was one of three guests at an Indonesian restaurant where 13 dishes were presented in addition to the rice. For a party of six, plan on yellow rice plus about a dozen or more selections which can include soup and prawn crackers.

The second time I had rijstafel was on the island of Ambon. I'd approached a bank to change money. It was closed but the bank manager heard me banging on the door, opened it and, during the exchange, invited me to his home where his charming wife offered me coffee and gifts of Indonesian batik fabrics and shirts. I wanted to reciprocate. 'Let me take you to lunch,' I cried, embarrassed by such spontaneous generosity. My host had a home telephone (unused then in Ambon, which is not on the usual tourist trail). He called a restaurant and 20 minutes later we sat at a table with his wife and three small children. The dishes kept coming, on and on, until there were about 20 in total. Despite my offer, my host insisted that he should pay as I was a guest in his country. Hospitality is integral to Indonesian culture, even to those who have little or nothing.) If you visit Indonesia, please give back something to those who welcome you so warmly.

A rijstafel is a balanced combination of many dishes and yellow rice. Dishes may include satay, a soup, appetisers (maybe meatballs and/or Indonesian spring rolls), at least one vegetable dish, one of fish, a curry, a salad, a sambal, and desserts such as banana fritters and fresh fruit. An egg curry is particularly appropriate and provides a tasty contrast in a rijstafel. To make an egg curry use any curry base in this book and allocate at least one boiled, shelled egg per person. Add a couple more for those who

would like seconds. It's advisable to prepare a curry a day or two in advance. Store it covered in the refrigerator then reheat it after the flavours have blended and matured.

No special tools are required to prepare Indonesian food in a reasonably well-equipped western kitchen, but a Chinese wok, and a mortar and pestle or food processor for grinding spices are time-savers. Fresh chillies are integral to many Indonesian dishes. Wear plastic disposable gloves when preparing chillies and keep your hands away from your eyes and face as the burning sting is unbearable.

With food serve light beer, fruit juice, weak, unsweetened Chinese tea (which Indonesians take solely with their meals) or soft drinks. If authenticity isn't essential, a mild, dry, inexpensive white wine would be appropriate. Indonesian food flavours are so strong that they diminish the quality of a top wine. Serve water at the table to cool palates stimulated by spicy dishes.

An Indonesian family meal may include rice and up to four dishes. However many Indonesian families exist on rice with a sambal or curry sauce and as many vegetables as can be found. Butter and cheese are not served. Beef is served if it is available – every bit of the cow is used; not just the meat. Do be sensitive to any Muslim guests' beliefs.

Do not include a pork dish if any guests are Muslims for although they could avoid eating it, many Muslims would consider it an insult that the cook has even considered preparing a pork dish. Some Muslims are so strict that if they believe pork has been previously cooked in a pot or pan they will not eat even the non-pork dishes cooked in that pan.

If you are on holiday in Indonesia and you are invited to dinner at the home of a local Indonesian, it is good form to bring a small gift such as chocolates or souvenirs from home, or sweets for the children. Wear neat, casual dress, not a t-shirt nor a sarong over a swimsuit. The hostess will be dressed in her best and may place her hands together, as if in Christian prayer, and bow her head in greeting. It would be polite for you to do the same.

It is quite polite in Indonesia to arrive at a private dinner party at least 10 minutes late. Usually, this is so that the hostess has had time to dress and look as radiant as

possible after spending so much time preparing the meal. Traditional Indonesian families refrain from conversing during the meal; talk is reserved for afterwards. Guests should take a small serve at first because the hosts' expectations are that guests will enjoy the meal and want more. It is offensive to the cook for a guest to request extra condiments or sauces as the dishes should be perfectly flavoured and not require any extra seasoning. You should never eat with or pass something with your left hand, as this is considered unclean. Use the fingertips of your right hand to eat, which is actually quite an art. If each table place is set with a soup bowl, plate, fork and spoon, do use them. Dessert and/or fruit are served after the main repast and an extra plate is usually provided for this.

The diversity of food and styles in Indonesia is truly amazing. This selection of recipes is just a small taste of what the country has to offer. 'Selamat masak dan selamat makan!' (Happy cooking and happy eating!)

Starters

Starters
Tempt Your Appetite

When wandering around Indonesia's street stalls, it is possible to eat a full and satisfying meal comprising completely of 'starters' which are supplied by hawkers at their warungs or little makeshift places. The warungs may be nothing more than plastic sheets over a tiny area, protecting pots and stoves from tropical rain. Diners wait while the food is cooked freshly before them. When the food is ready the diners sit on a wooden stool beside the warung to eat.

As in China, Vietnam, Malaysia, Thailand and Cambodia, and indeed the whole of Asia, street food is cheap and tasty. The atmosphere is particularly exciting at night when a whole food culture emerges. Families and friends gather together, chatting, picking, listening to any background music and getting up from chairs or mats for more appetisers if hunger pangs still gnaw.

In your own home, the environment will tend to be more formal as you present one or several of the following dishes to tantalise your guests with the tastes of Indonesia. That is unless you set your dinner party date for an evening by the barbecue outdoors. Spring rolls, fritters, wontons, satays, morsels of chicken and fish cakes can comprise a whole meal when served with vegetables, the staple ingredient of rice and a salad.

We suggest that home cooks choose one or two of the following starters to welcome guests to a meal redolent with spices and smoky aromas. Then continue the banquet as casually or formally as you wish.

Spring Rolls (Lumpia Goreng)

Makes about 24

1 tablespoon peanut oil

2 cloves garlic, crushed

4 spring onions (scallions), sliced

350 g (12 oz) chicken mince

1 carrot, finely sliced

2 cups (8 oz/225 g) Chinese cabbage, shredded

2 tablespoons sweet soy sauce (kecap manis)

50 g (1¾ oz) vermicelli noodles, cooked

Spring roll wrappers

Oil, for cooking

SPRING ROLL SAUCE

1 tablespoons tamarind concentrate

1 tablespoon soy sauce

2 tablespoons water

1/2 teaspoon sambal ulek

1/2 teaspoon root ginger, grated (shredded)

1/2 teaspoon palm sugar or brown sugar

Heat the peanut oil in a wok or frying pan. Add the garlic, shallots and chicken mince and stir-fry for 4–5 minutes, or until the mince is cooked. Add the carrot, cabbage and kecap manis and stir-fry for 3–4 minutes, or until cooked. Combine the noodles with the chicken and leave to cool. Place 1 tablespoon of mixture on a spring roll wrapper. Roll up and brush the ends with water.

Heat the oil in a wok or frying pan. Add the spring rolls to the work and fry for 1–2 minutes, or until golden and crisp.

Combine all the sauce ingredients in a small dish and set aside.

Drain on kitchen paper and serve with spring roll sauce.

Corn Fritters (Perkedel Jagung)

Makes about 16

14 oz (400 g) can sweet corn kernels, drained
1 small red chilli, deseeded and finely chopped
4 spring onions (scallions), sliced
1 teaspoon ground coriander
Pinch of salt
1 egg
1/4 cup (1 oz/30 g) rice flour
1 tablespoon plain (all-purpose) flour
Vegetable oil, for cooking
Soy sauce, to serve

In a bowl, combine the corn kernels, chilli, shallots, coriander, salt, egg and flours and mix well. Leave to stand for 30 minutes.

Heat the oil in a wok or frying pan. Drop spoonfuls of mixture into the oil and cook until golden. Serve with soy sauce.

Indonesian Beef Croquettes (Perkedel Daging)

PANCAKES

1 1/2 cups (6 oz/150 g) plain (all-purpose) flour

2 eggs, separated

2 cups (16 fl oz/475 ml) water

Pinch of salt

Peanut oil, for cooking

1 cup (4 oz/115 g) breadcrumbs

FILLING

1 tablespoons peanut oil

1 brown onion, finely chopped

2 garlic cloves, crushed

14 oz (400 g) beef mince

1–2 teaspoons chilli powder

1 tablespoon sweet soy sauce (kecap manis)

2 cups (8 oz/225 g) cabbage, finely shredded

Spring roll sauce, to serve (see recipe)

To make the pancakes, whisk together the flour, egg yolks, water and salt in a mixing bowl to make a batter.

Heat a little oil in a frying pan, just enough to coat. Tip a small amount of the batter into the frying pan to cover the surface, making them paper thin. Cook the pancakes one at a time. Cook one side only. When the batter starts to colour, remove from the frying pan. Tip onto a warmed plate to keep warm while you cook the rest of the pancakes. Cover with kitchen foil.

To make the filling, heat the oil in a frying pan. Add the onion, garlic and beef mince and fry for 4–5 minutes, or until meat is cooked through. Add the chilli powder, soy sauce and cabbage and cook for another 2–3 minutes. Leave the mixture to cool.

Meanwhile, beat the egg whites in a wide bowl. Place the breadcrumbs on a plate. Place tablespoons of filling on each pancake. Fold to form an envelope. Dip the pancakes in the beaten egg whites and then into the breadcrumbs.

Heat the oil in a wok and cook the pancakes for 1–2 minutes, or until golden and crisp. Drain on paper towel. Serve with spring roll sauce.

Pineapple and Rum Turkey Kebabs (Ayam Belanda Nanas)

12 bamboo skewers

13 oz (375 g) turkey breast tenderloin steaks or boneless turkey breast

1 medium onion, peeled and cut into thin wedges

2 nectarines, peeled, or 3 plums, pitted, and cut into thick slices

1 1/2 cups (10 oz/280 g) fresh or canned pineapple chunks

Hot cooked rice (optional), to serve

MARINADE

1/3 cup (2½ fl oz/75 ml) unsweetened pineapple juice

3 tablespoons rum

1 tablespoon brown sugar

1 tablespoon lemongrass, finely chopped or 2 teaspoons lemon peel, finely shredded

1 tablespoon olive oil

Soak the bamboo skewers in cold water for 15–20 minutes.

Cut the turkey into 1 in (2.5 cm) cubes and put them in a clean plastic bag set in a shallow dish.

To make the marinade, combine the pineapple juice, rum, brown sugar, lemongrass and oil in a bowl and mix to combine. Pour the marinade over the turkey and close the bag. Marinate in the refrigerator for 4–24 hours, turning occasionally.

Drain the turkey, reserving the marinade. In a small saucepan bring the marinade to the boil. Remove from the heat.

Onto four skewers each 12 in (30 cm) long, alternately thread a piece of turkey and then a piece of onion. Grill (broil) the kebabs on the rack of an uncovered grill (broiler) on medium heat for 12–14 minutes, or until the turkey is cooked but still tender, turning once and brushing occasionally with marinade.

Meanwhile, on another four kebab skewers, alternately thread the nectarines and pineapple chunks. Place on the grill rack next to the turkey kebabs for the last 5 minutes of grilling, turning and brushing once with marinade. Serve with rice, if desired.

CRISPY SEAFOOD WONTONS (PANGSIT GORENG)

3½ oz (100 g) peeled green shrimp
(prawns)
200 g fish fillets, skinned and diced
1 garlic clove, crushed
2 green shallots, sliced
2 teaspoons soy sauce
1 egg
1 packet wonton skins
Peanut oil, for cooking

WONTON SAUCE

2 tablespoons soy sauce
2 tablespoons water
1 garlic clove, crushed
$1/2$ teaspoon root ginger, grated
(shredded)
$1/2$ teaspoon palm sugar or brown sugar

Combine the shrimp, fish, garlic, shallots, soy sauce and egg in a food processor. Process mixture until smooth.

Place spoonfuls of mixture in the centre of each wonton skin. Brush the edges with a little water. Fold the skin in half to form a triangle and press the edges lightly to seal.

Combine the ingredients for the sauce in a small dish and set aside.

Heat the oil in a wok and cook each wonton for 1–2 minutes, or until golden and crisp. Serve with wonton sauce.

Chicken Satay (Sate Ayam)

Makes about 12

12 bamboo skewers
1 lb 2 oz (500 g) chicken thigh fillets, diced
   (beef, lamb and pork can also be used)
2 tablespoons peanut oil
2 tablespoons sweet soy sauce (kecap manis)
1 tablespoon soy sauce
1 garlic clove, crushed
Peanut sauce, to serve (see recipe)

Soak the bamboo skewers in cold water for 15–20 minutes.

Thread diced chicken onto the bamboo skewers. Arrange in a large, shallow dish.

Combine the peanut oil, soy sauces and garlic in a bowl and stir to combine. Pour the marinade over the chicken and leave to marinate in the refrigerator for 1–2 hours.

Cook the satays on a barbecue for 10–15 minutes, or until cooked through.

Serve with peanut sauce.

Spicy Meatballs (Rempah Daging)

Makes about 20

2 shallots, chopped
2 garlic cloves, chopped
2 teaspoons cumin seeds
1 teaspoon ground coriander
1 lb 2 oz (500 g) beef mince
1/2 cup (2 oz/60 g) fresh breadcrumbs
1 egg yolk
2 teaspoons sambal ulek
1 tablespoon soy sauce
1/4 cup (2 fl oz/60 ml) peanut oil
Wedges of lime, to serve
Sweet chilli sauce, to serve (optional)

Crush or pound together the shallots, garlic, cumin seeds and coriander in a mortar with a pestle or in a small food processor.

Combine the mixture with the beef, breadcrumbs, egg yolk, sambal ulek and soy sauce. Shape into walnut-sized balls.

Heat the oil in a large frying pan. Fry the meatballs for 5–6 minutes, or until golden. Serve with wedges of lime and/or sweet chilli sauce.

Spicy Fish Fritters (Perkedel Ikan)

Makes about 16

4 spring onions (scallions), sliced

2 garlic cloves, chopped

2 teaspoons root ginger, chopped

1 lb 2 oz (500 g) boneless fish fillets

1 tablespoon soy sauce

2 teaspoons sweet soy sauce (kecap manis)

1 egg

1 tablespoon cornflour (corn starch)

Peanut oil, for cooking

DIPPING SAUCE

1 tablespoon sweet soy sauce

2 tablespoons soy sauce

$1/2$ teaspoon sambal oelek

Combine the shallots, garlic, ginger, fish, soy sauce, kecap manis, egg and cornflour in a food processor. Process until the mixture comes together and is smooth.

Using wet hands shape the mixture into small patties (the mixture tends to be wet) and put on a plate. Cover with cling film (plastic wrap) and let stand for 30 minutes to 1 hour in the refrigerator.

Heat the oil in a non-stick frying pan or wok. Cook the patties for 1–2 minutes on each side, or until golden.

Combine the ingredients for dipping sauce in a small dish. Serve the fritters with dipping sauce.

Chicken

Chicken
Out for a Duck

Chicken and duck are the least expensive meats available in Indonesia, so Indonesians have drawn on all sorts of foreign-influenced recipes to make poultry presentable and tasty.

In Indonesia there are always a few chickens wandering around village houses, no matter how poor the household. Ducks are a bit more hard to obtain, but any of the following recipes can be prepared with duck if you happen to have bought one. Just allow a little more cooking time for duck.

Indonesians fry, sauté, grill, stew or oven-bake chicken as enthusiastically as we do in the West but the taste sensations differ with the cooking traditions from Java, Bali and Jakarta – and their wonderful spices. Whether in a curry or in coconut milk, or cooked Chinese-style with soy sauce, chicken is tasty, cheap and chock-a-block full of goodness, particularly if the skin is removed. *Ayam goreng* (fried chicken) is a national dish and is fairly easy to prepare.

If you are pushed for preparation time, pick up a barbecued chicken from your nearest outlet and substitute it in the following recipes.

Ideally prepare your dishes in advance and refrigerate overnight before reheating and serving. The spicy flavours will be even tastier.

SPICED CHICKEN DRUMETTES (AYAM GORENG)

Oil, for greasing and spraying
$1/2$ cup (2 oz/60 g) cornflour (corn starch)
2 teaspoons ground black pepper
$1/2$ teaspoon salt
1 teaspoon ground coriander
1 teaspoon ground cumin
$1/2$ teaspoon ground chilli powder
2 lb 4 oz (1 kg) chicken drumsticks
Sambal kepac (see recipe) or light soy sauce, to serve

Preheat the oven to 200°C/400°F/Gas mark 6. Lightly grease a non-stick baking sheet with oil.

Combine the cornflour, pepper, salt, coriander, cumin and chilli powder in a mixing bowl. Toss the chicken in the spice mixture to thoroughly coat.

Place the chicken on the prepared baking sheet, spray lightly with oil and bake for 20–25 minutes, or until golden and crisp. Serve with *sambal kecap* or light soy sauce.

Javanese Curried Chicken (Ayam Jawa)

Serves 4

2 tablespoons vegetable oil

4 chicken thighs

1 onion, chopped

3 garlic cloves, crushed

1 stick lemongrass, finely chopped

1 teaspoon root ginger, grated (crushed)

1 teaspoon ground coriander

1 teaspoon ground turmeric

$1/2$ teaspoon ground cumin

1 cup (8 fl oz/250 ml) coconut milk

6 curry leaves

$1/2$ cup coriander (cilantro) leaves

Nasi putih, to serve (see recipe)

Heat the oil in a frying pan. Add the chicken and cook for 4–5 minutes, or until golden. Add the onion, garlic, lemongrass and ginger. Cook until the onion is soft, about 5 minutes. Add the ground coriander, turmeric and cumin and cook until aromatic.

Add the coconut milk and curry leaves and simmer uncovered for 15–20 minutes, or until the sauce has thickened. Stir through the coriander leaves. Serve with *nasi putih*.

Spicy Chicken Soup (Soto Ayam)

3¼ lb (1.5 kg) whole chicken

2 teaspoons salt

2 tablespoons chicken stock powder

3½ oz (100 g) vermicelli noodles

1 tablespoon peanut oil

2 garlic, cloves crushed

2 teaspoons root ginger, grated (crushed)

1 stalk lemongrass, white part finely
   chopped and top part tied in a knot

1 teaspoon ground turmeric

2 teaspoons ground coriander

2 lime leaves, finely sliced

Juice of 1 lime

Lime wedges, to serve

Sambal kepac or sambal cuka (see
   recipes), to serve

GARNISHES

4 green shallots, sliced

1 cup (4 oz/115 g) beansprouts, trimmed

2 hard-boiled eggs, quartered

2 potatoes, cooked and sliced

Place the chicken in a large saucepan. Cover with water, add the salt and bring to the boil. Reduce the heat, cover and simmer for 30–35 minutes, or until the chicken is cooked through. Remove the chicken and strain the liquid, reserving 6 cups (2½ pints/1.4 litres). Stir in chicken the stock powder.

Remove the skin and bones from chicken and shred the flesh.

Cook the noodles according to the packet directions. Drain and set aside.

Heat the oil in a large saucepan. Add the garlic, ginger and lemongrass and cook for 1–2 minutes. Add the turmeric and coriander and cook until aromatic.

Add the reserved stock, chicken and lime leaves. Simmer for 10 minutes. Add the lime juice just before serving.

Divide the noodles between serving bowls. Spoon the chicken soup over the noodles and top with garnishes. Serve with wedges of lime, *sambal kecap* or *sambal cuka*.

Javanese Chicken and Vegetables (Ayam Jawa Sayur)

Serves 4

2 tablespoons peanut oil
1 lb 2 oz (500 g) chicken thigh fillets
3 shallots, sliced
2 garlic cloves, crushed
2 teaspoons root ginger, grated (crushed)
1 teaspoon ground turmeric
1 teaspoon ground coriander
1 teaspoon ground cumin
1 teaspoon galangal powder
1 cup (8 fl oz/250 ml) coconut milk

3/4 cup (6 fl oz/175 ml) chicken stock
2 teaspoons sambal ulek
1 stalk lemongrass, bruised
2 salam leaves (use curry leaves or bay as an alternative)
1 carrot, sliced
2 potatoes, diced
5 oz (150 g) green (French) beans, sliced
Nasi putih (see recipe), to serve

Heat the oil in a large saucepan. Add the chicken and cook for 4–5 minutes, or until golden. Add the shallots, garlic and ginger. Cook until the shallots are soft. Add the turmeric, coriander, cumin and galangal powder. Cook until aromatic.

Add the coconut milk, chicken stock, sambal ulek, lemongrass and salam leaves. Bring to the boil. Add the vegetables and cook for 10–15 minutes, or until the vegetables are tender. Serve with *nasi putih*.

Chicken in Coconut Milk (Opor Ayam)

2 tablespoons peanut oil
8 small chicken pieces
2 onions, sliced
2 teaspoons ground coriander
1 teaspoon ground cumin
1/2 teaspoon galangal powder
1 1/2 cups (12 fl oz/350 ml) coconut cream
1 1/2 cups (12 fl oz/350 ml) coconut milk
4 kaffir lime leaves, thinly sliced
Nasi putih (see recipe), to serve

PASTE
2 garlic cloves
2 teaspoons root ginger, chopped
1 teaspoon shrimp paste (terasi)
3 candle nuts (or macadamia nuts)
1–2 small red chillis, deseeded
1/2 teaspoon salt

Crush or pound the paste ingredients in a mortar with a pestle or in a food processor.

Heat the oil in a large saucepan. Add the chicken and cook for 4–5 minutes, or until golden. Remove the chicken and set aside.

Add the onions to the pan and cook for 3–4 minutes, or until brown. Add the paste and cook for 1–2 minutes. Add the coriander, cumin and galangal powder and cook until aromatic.

Add the coconut cream, coconut milk, lime leaves and chicken. Bring to the boil, reduce the heat and simmer for 20–30 minutes, or until chicken is tender and sauce has reduced. Serve with *nasi putih*.

Roast Spiced Chicken (Ayam Panggang Pedis)

Serve 4

2 tablespoons margarine
2 garlic cloves, crushed
2 tablespoons sweet soy sauce (kecap manis)
2 tablespoons tamarind concentrate
2–3 teaspoons sambal ulek
3¼ lb (1.5 kg) chicken, cleaned
Wedges of lime, to serve

Preheat the oven to 200°C/400°F/Gas mark 6.

Heat the margarine in a small saucepan. Add the garlic and cook for 1–2 minutes. Add the kecap manis, tamarind and sambal ulek. Bring to the boil. Remove from the heat and brush over the chicken.

Place the chicken on a rack over a baking dish. Cover lightly with foil and bake for 30 minutes. Remove the foil, baste the chicken and bake for another 20–30 minutes, or until cooked.

Cut the chicken into pieces and serve with lime wedges.

INDONESIAN CURRY (KARI INDONESIA)

Serves 5

1 tablespoon fresh ginger, grated (crushed)

1 teaspoon turmeric

1 teaspoon salt

1 teaspoon sugar

3¼–4½ lb (1.5–2 kg) chicken, cut into pieces

4 teaspoons vegetable oil

2 medium onions, cut into very thin wedges

1 bay leaf

14 oz (400 g) can coconut milk

1½ kaffir lime leaves or 1 teaspoon grated (shredded) lime peel

1 tablespoon chopped fresh coriander (cilantro)

Cooked rice, to serve

Soy sauce, to serve

CURRY PASTE

2 medium onions, cut into chunks

2 large garlic cloves

2 teaspoons Madras curry powder

1½ teaspoon coriander

½ teaspoon cinnamon

½ teaspoon ground red pepper

GARNISH

Coriander (cilantro) leaves, sliced spring onions (scallions), peanuts, sliced hot fresh chillies

Combine the ginger, turmeric, salt, and sugar in a bowl; add the chicken and toss well to coat. Cover and marinate in the refrigerator for up to 24 hours.

Heat 2 teaspoons of oil in a deep 12 in (30 cm) skillet over medium-high heat. Add the onion wedges and bay leaf and cook for 8 minutes until browned. Transfer to plate andset aside.

Meanwhile, to make the curry paste, purée the onion chunks, garlic, 2 tablespoons water, curry powder, coriander, cinnamon and red pepper in blender until smooth.

Heat the remaining 2 teaspoons of oil in the skillet over medium-high heat; add the curry paste and cook for 4–5 minutes, stirring occasionally, until thickened. Add the chicken and coat with paste. Cover and simmer for 10 minutes. Stir in the coconut milk, onions and lime leaves. Simmer uncovered for 20 minutes more until the chicken is cooked through. Remove the bay leaf. Divide between serving plates. Serve with rice, soy sauce and garnishes.

CRISPY FRIED DUCK (BEBEK GORENG)

Serves 4

2 tablespoons soy sauce
1 tablespoon tamarind concentrate
1 tablespoon peanut oil
1 teaspoon root ginger, grated (crushed)
1 garlic clove, crushed
1 teaspoon ground coriander
4 duck breasts
1/4 cup (2 fl oz/60 ml) peanut oil, for cooking
Salad greens, to serve

In a bowl, combine the soy sauce, tamarind, oil, ginger, garlic and coriander to make a marinade. Place the duck in a shallow non-metallic container and pour the marinade over the top. Leave to marinate in the refrigerator for 2–3 hours.

Preheat the oven to 200°C/400°F/Gas mark 6.

Heat the oil in a frying pan. Add the duck and cook for 1–2 minutes or until golden and crisp. Place the duck on a rack set over a shallow baking dish and cook for 15–18 minutes. Slice and serve with salad greens.

Grilled Chicken (Ayam Panggang)

Serves 4–6

2 tablespoons peanut oil
1/3 cup (2½ fl oz/75 ml) soy sauce
2 tablespoons lime juice
2 tablespoons lime zest
2 teaspoons sambal ulek
2 garlic cloves, crushed
1 tablespoon palm sugar or brown sugar
8 chicken thigh fillets, trimmed
Cooked rice, to serve
Green vegetables, to serve
Sweet chilli sauce, to serve

Combine the oil, soy sauce, lime juice, lime zest, sambal ulek, garlic and sugar in a bowl. Place the chicken in a non-metallic dish. Pour the marinade over and leave to marinate in the refrigerator for 2–3 hours.

Cook the chicken on a barbecue plate for 10–15 minutes, occasionally basting. Serve with cooked rice, green vegetables and sweet chilli sauce (on the side).

Chicken and Corn Soup (Sop Ayam Jagung)

Serves 4

2 teaspoons peanut oil
6 cups (2½ pints/1.5 litres) chicken stock
3 cups (1 lb/450 g) shredded cooked chicken
400 g (14 oz) can sweet corn kernels, drained
2 tablespoons sweet soy sauce (kecap manis)
1–2 teaspoons sambal ulek
2 cups (8 oz/225 g) shredded English or Chinese spinach, washed and drained
Salt, to taste

PASTE
2 French shallots, chopped
2 cloves garlic
2 candle nuts (or macadamias)
1 teaspoon terasi
2 teaspoons peanut oil

Crush or pound the paste ingredients in a mortar with pestle or use a small food processor.

Heat the peanut oil in a large saucepan. Add the paste and fry for 1–2 minutes. Add the stock, chicken, corn, kecap manis and sambal ulek. Bring to the boil and simmer over low heat for 5–10 minutes.

Add the spinach and cook for 1–2 minutes. Season with salt. Divide between soup bowls.

BALINESE-STYLE FRIED CHICKEN (AYAM BALI)

Serves 4

1/4 cup (2 fl oz/60 ml) peanut oil

8 small chicken pieces

3/4–1 cup (6–8 fl oz/175–250 ml) coconut
  milk

2 teaspoons sweet soy sauce (kecap
  manis)

2 tablespoons lime juice

2 tablespoons lime zest

1 long green chilli, deseeded and sliced

Rice, to serve

Green (French) beans, to serve

PASTE

3 shallots

2 cloves garlic

2 teaspoons root ginger, chopped

4 medium red chillies, deseeded and
  chopped

3 candle nuts (or macadamias)

2 teaspoons sweet soy sauce (kecap
  manis)

Crush or pound the paste ingredients, except for the kecap manis, in a mortar with
pestle or in a food processor. Add the kecap manis and stir to combine.

Heat the oil in a wok or frying pan. Add the chicken in two batches and cook until
golden.

Remove the chicken and drain on kitchen paper. Pour off and discard the excess oil.

Cook the paste for 1–2 minutes. Add the coconut milk, kecap manis, lemon juice
zest, chilli and chicken. Simmer for 25–30 minutes or until the chicken is tender. Serve
with cooked long grain rice and green beans.

MARINATED CHICKEN WITH SNOW PEAS
(AYAM DIASINKAN DENGAN KACANG KAPRI)

Serves 4

2 garlic cloves, crushed
2 teaspoons root ginger, grated (crushed)
1 lemongrass stalk, finely chopped
2 tablespoons soy sauce
1 teaspoon sambal ulek
1 tablespoons sweet soy sauce (kecap manis)
2 teaspoons sesame oil
1 lb 2 oz (500 g) chicken thigh fillets, thinly sliced
1 tablespoons peanut oil
5 oz (150 g) snow peas (mange tout), trimmed and halved
8 oz (230 g) can bamboo shoots, drained
Rice, to serve

Combine the garlic, ginger, lemongrass, soy sauce, sambal ulek, kecap manis and sesame oil in a shallow dish to make a marinade. Add the chicken and coat well. Leave to marinate for
1–2 hours.

Heat the oil in a wok or frying pan. Add the chicken (reserving the marinade) and stir-fry for 4–5 minutes, or until golden. Add the marinade, snow peas and bamboo shoots and stir-fry for 2–3 minutes or until the snow peas are cooked. Add a little water if the sauce becomes too thick. Divide between dishes.

Meat

Meat
Tough it Out

Indonesians regard beef as food with which to celebrate a special occasion. It is expensive and not usually daily fare. Pork, on the other hand, is a big winner in Bali where it is popular with Hindus and Christians.

Meat is of higher quality in the West than it is in Indonesia so you can go ahead with enthusiasm in preparing the following dishes. These dishes can be served with rice or noodles and vegetables to make a satisfying family meal. Otherwise, one dish could make up part of your Indonesian dinner party with exciting Indonesian flavours.

Diced Spicy Beef (Empal Daging)

1¾ lb (750 g) beef, thinly sliced

2 tablespoons peanut oil

1 bunch snake beans, trimmed
   into 2 in (5 cm) pieces.

1/2 cup (4 fl oz/125 ml) water

Boiled rice, to serve

PASTE

1 teaspoon coriander seeds

3 garlic cloves, chopped

2 teaspoons galangal, chopped

1 teaspoon palm sugar or brown sugar

2 tablespoons tamarind concentrate

1/4 cup (4 fl oz/125 ml) soy sauce

GARNISH

Toasted desiccated (dry unsweetened
   shredded) coconut

Crush or pound the dry paste ingredients in a mortar and pestle or food processor. Crush until a paste has formed. Add tamarind and soy sauce.

Marinate the beef in the paste in a non-metallic container for 1–2 hours in the refrigerator.

Heat oil in a wok. Add beef and stir-fry for 4–5 minutes. Add beans and cook for 3–4 minutes or until beans are tender. Add a little water if the sauce is too thick. Garnish with toasted coconut. Serve with boiled rice on the side.

Dry-Fried Beef Curry (Rendang Daging)

Serves 4

1/4 cup (¾ oz/20 g) desiccated (dry
   unsweetened shredded) coconut
1 1/2 tablespoons vegetable oil
2 1/4 lb (1 kg) beef, diced
2 cups (16 fl oz/475 ml) coconut milk
2 salam leaves
1 stalk lemongrass, white part chopped
   and the top tied in a knot
Boiled rice, to serve

PASTE
3 shallots, chopped
6–8 medium red chillies, deseeded and
   chopped
2 teaspoons root ginger, chopped
3 garlic cloves, chopped
1/2 teaspoon galangal powder
1 teaspoon ground turmeric
2 teaspoons peanut oil (see method)

Crush or pound the paste ingredients in a mortar with pestle, or in a food processor. (Add 2 teaspoons peanut oil if using a food processor).

Dry-fry the desiccated coconut in a saucepan until golden.

Heat 1 tablespoon oil in a large frying pan. Add half the beef and stir-fry 2–3 minutes, or until the beef is brown. Remove and set aside. Add the remaining oil and beef and stir-fry for another 2–3 minutes. Remove and set aside. Add the paste and stir-fry for 1 minute.

Add the coconut milk, salam leaves, lemongrass stalk and beef. Bring to the boil. Reduce the heat and simmer uncovered for 1 1/2 hours and or until the liquid has evaporated and beef is tender. Serve with boiled rice on the side.

Pork in Soy Sauce (Babi Kecap)

1 tablespoon peanut oil
1 lb 2 oz (500 g) pork fillet, sliced
1 onion, sliced
3 garlic cloves, crushed
1 teaspoon root ginger, grated (crushed)

1/4 cup (2 fl oz/60 ml) sweet soy sauce
 (kecap manis)
2 tablespoons water
4 spring onions (scallions), sliced
Boiled rice, to serve

Heat the oil in a wok. Add the pork and stir-fry for 5–6 minutes, or until golden. Add the onions and garlic and stir-fry for 2–3 minutes. Add the ginger, kecap manis, water and spring onions and cook for 2–3 minutes. Serve with side bowls of boiled rice.

Beef Liver in Coconut Milk (Kalio Hati)

1 lb 6 oz (600 g) beef liver, well trimmed,
 sliced and cut into 3/4 in (2 cm) squares
3 cups (24 fl oz/750 ml) coconut milk
1 teaspoon salt
Boiled rice, to serve

PASTE
8 shallots, peeled and sliced
3 garlic cloves, peeled and sliced

14 bird's eye chillies, sliced
3/8 in (1 cm) galangal, peeled and sliced
3/8 in (1 cm) fresh turmeric, peeled and
 sliced
3/8 in (1 cm) piece of root ginger, peeled
 and sliced
2 tablespoons oil
1 lemongrass, bruised
2 kaffir lime leaves

To make the paste, grind all the ingredients except the oil, lemongrass and lime leaves. Heat oil in a wok and fry the paste along with lemongrass and lime leaves for 2–3 minutes.

Add liver and sauté for 2 minutes. Add coconut milk and salt and simmer, uncovered, until liver is tender and sauce has thickened. Serve with side bowls of boiled rice.

BALINESE PORK (BABI BALI)

1 tablespoon peanut oil
1¾ lb (750 g) pork loin or fillet, diced
1/4 cup (2 fl oz/60 ml) sweet soy sauce (kecap manis)
1 tablespoon lime juice
1–1 1/2 cups (12 fl oz/750 ml) water
Boiled rice, to serve

PASTE
3 small red chillies, deseeded and chopped
2 shallots, chopped
2 garlic cloves, chopped
2 teaspoons root ginger, chopped
1 teaspoon shrimp paste (terasi)
2 teaspoons peanut oil

Crush or pound the paste ingredients in a mortar with pestle or use a food processor.

Heat the oil in a saucepan and stir-fry the paste for 1–2 minutes. Add the pork and stir-fry for 4–5 minutes. Add the kecap manis, lime juice and water. Cover the saucepan and simmer for 1 hour. Serve with side bowls of boiled rice.

INDONESIAN PORK SPARE RIBS
(BABI TULANG CIN)

Serves 4

1¾ lb (750 g) pork spare ribs
1^1/$_2$ tablespoons peanut oil
1 teaspoon ground coriander
^{1}/$_2$ teaspoon ground cumin
^{1}/$_2$ teaspoon ground pepper
2 tablespoons soy sauce
1 tablespoon tamarind concentrate
1 teaspoon brown sugar
^{1}/$_4$ cup (2 fl oz/60 ml) water
Chinese greens, to serve
Boiled rice, to serve

PASTE
2 shallots, chopped
2 garlic cloves
2 teaspoons root ginger, chopped

Crush or pound the paste ingredients in a mortar with pestle or use a small food processor.

Chop the spare ribs in half. Heat 1 tablespoon of the oil in a wok or frying pan. Add the spare ribs and fry for 2–3 minutes, or until the ribs are golden and crisp. Remove and set aside.

Heat the remaining oil and add the paste. Stir-fry for 1 minute. Add coriander, cumin, pepper, soy sauce, tamarind and sugar. Return the ribs to the sauce and simmer, covered, for 10 minutes, or until the ribs are cooked through. Add a little water if the sauce becomes too thick. Serve with Chinese greens and side bowl of rice.

Lamb Cooked with Tomatoes (Kambing Masak Tomato)

Serves 4

1 tablespoon vegetable oil
4 lamb chops, trimmed
1 onion, sliced
14 oz (400 g) can diced tomatoes
1/2 cup (4 fl oz/125 ml) beef stock
1 stalk lemongrass, bruised
2 potatoes, peeled and diced
Boiled rice, to serve

PASTE
2 garlic cloves, chopped
4 medium chillies, deseeded and chopped
Pinch of salt

Crush or pound the paste ingredients in a mortar with pestle or use a food processor.

Heat the oil in a large saucepan. Add the chops and fry for 2–3 minutes on each side, or until brown. Remove and set aside. Add the onion and cook for 2–3 minutes.

Add the paste to the saucepan and cook for 1–2 minutes. Add the tomatoes, stock, lemongrass, potatoes and chops. Cover and simmer for 30–40 minutes, or until the chops are tender and sauce has reduced. Serve with boiled rice.

BARBECUED LAMB CUTLETS (KAMBING PANGGANG)

Serves 4

2 tablespoons peanut oil
¼ cup (2 fl oz/60 ml) lemon juice
1 tablespoon soy sauce
2 garlic cloves, crushed
1 teaspoon ground coriander
1 teaspoon ground cumin
8 lamb cutlets
Nasi goreng (see recipe), to serve
Peanut sauce (see recipe), to serve

Combine the oil, lemon juice, soy sauce, garlic, coriander and cumin to make the marinade. Place the lamb cutlets in a non-metallic dish. Pour the marinade over and marinate in the refrigerator for 2–3 hours.

Cook the lamb cutlets on a barbecue plate for 8–10 minutes, occasionally basting. Serve with nasi goreng and peanut sauce.

Beef in Tamarind (Daging Asam)

Serves 4

1 tablespoon peanut oil, extra
1 3/4 lb (750 g) rump beef, diced
3 spring onions (scallions), sliced
2 medium red chillies, deseeded and sliced
1 tablespoon sweet soy sauce (kecap manis)
1 tablespoon tamarind concentrate
1/2–3/4 cup (6–8 fl oz/175–250 ml) beef stock
1 eggplant (aubergine), diced
Boiled rice, to serve

PASTE
2 shallots, chopped
2 garlic cloves, chopped
1/2 teaspoon terasi
2 teaspoons peanut oil

Crush or pound the paste ingredients in a mortar with a pestle or use a food processor.

Heat the oil in a wok or saucepan. Add the beef and stir-fry for 3–4 minutes, or until brown. Add the paste and spring onions and stir-fry for 2–3 minutes. Add the chillies, kecap manis, tamarind and stock. Reduce the heat, cover and simmer for 10 minutes. Add the eggplant and cook for another 5–6 minutes, or until the beef is tender and the sauce has reduced. Stir through and serve with side bowls of boiled rice.

Seafood

Seafood
Spicy Hot or Coconut Cream

Pontianak and Samarinda in Kalimantan have enormous river shrimp, while Jayapura offers Indonesia's best selection of barbecued fish. While the fish and seafood recipes to follow rely on fresh produce, many Indonesians rely on dried fish because of the lack of refrigeration in their communities.

Fresh fish is prepared in so many ways. It may be grilled (broiled) or barbecued over charcoals, wrapped in a banana leaf (or foil in your home kitchen) and baked, be it tuna, carp, mullet, bream or bass. Shellfish comes in the form of garlic-and-butter-sauced shrimp, which also make sensational satays, and West Javanese spiced shrimp balls. Also from Java comes otak-otak. In this dish, cooked shrimp are combined with double the amount of firm fish fillets along with chillies, spring onions (scallions), garlic, lemongrass, coriander (cilantro) and unsweetened coconut milk. This is divided among banana leaves (or foil) and baked, steamed or grilled. The result is a delicious fish paté.

Alternatively, one can make fish foil parcels from fish fillets, spices and coconut cream and quickly barbecue them over hot coals. Fish in soy sauce is popular in Sumatra. If you visit Ujung Pandang, the capital of Sulawesi, you'll find a huge variety of barbecued fish, including squid, prepared by the seafaring Bugis people at their numerous stalls.

Fish fillets fried then topped with a lime juice, soy sauce, coconut cream and vinegar sauce, are another delicious surprise for Westerners. Squid is popular in curry and is also fiery when cooked with dried chillies and shrimp paste. Other delicacies include lobster, crab and anchovies.

Sambal Fried Shrimp (Udang Goreng)

1 tablespoon vegetable oil
24 green shrimp, heads and shells removed
Nasi goreng (see recipe), to serve
Nasi putih (see recipe), to serve (optional)

PASTE

3 garlic cloves, chopped
3 medium chillies, deseeded and chopped
3 teaspoons root ginger, chopped
1 stalk lemongrass, chopped
1 teaspoon ground coriander
Pinch of salt
2 teaspoons vegetable oil

Crush or pound the paste ingredients in a mortar with a pestle or use a food processor.

Heat the oil in a wok or frying pan. Add the shrimp and paste, and stir-fry for 3–4 minutes, or until cooked.

Serve with nasi goreng or nasi putih.

Baked Fish with Spicy Soy Sauce (Ikan Kecap)

Serves 4

1lb 20 oz –2¼ lb (800 g–1 kg) whole snapper
2 teaspoons peanut oil
1 tablespoon lemon juice
Pinch of salt
Lemon slices
Boiled rice, to serve

SAUCE

2 teaspoons peanut oil
2 garlic cloves, crushed
2 teaspoons root ginger, grated (crushed)
1 small red chilli, deseeded and sliced
4 spring onions (scallions), sliced
2 tablespoons soy sauce
1 tablespoon sweet soy sauce (kecap manis)
1/2 cup (4 fl oz/125 ml) water

Preheat the oven to 200°C/400°F/Gas mark 6.

Make two diagonal cuts on each side of the fish, then brush with oil and lemon juice. Season with salt and place slices of lemon in the fish. Wrap the fish in baking paper and aluminium foil and place on a baking sheet. Bake in preheated oven for 30–40 minutes or until cooked.

To make the sauce, heat the oil in a small saucepan. Add the garlic, ginger, chilli and spring onions and cook for 1–2 minutes. Add the soy sauce, kecap manis and water and cook for 2–3 minutes.

When the fish is cooked, transfer it to a large serving dish and pour the sauce over. Serve with side bowls of boiled rice.

Calamari (Cumi-Cumi Goreng)

Serves 4

1/4 cup (2 fl oz/60 ml) lemon juice
1/2 teaspoon ground turmeric
1 garlic clove, crushed
Pinch of salt
1 lb 2 oz (500 g) squid
1/2 cup (2 oz/60 g) plain (all-purpose) flour
Oil, for cooking
Chilli flakes, to serve
Lemon or lime wedges, to serve

Combine lemon juice, turmeric, garlic and salt to make marinade.

Cut squid into rings or pieces. Place squid in a dish. Pour marinade over and marinate for 2–3 hours in the refrigerator.

Dip squid in flour and deep-fry in hot oil until golden and crisp.

Serve squid with chilli flakes and lemon or lime wedges.

Pan-Fried Fish (Ikan Goreng)

Serves 4

4 boneless fish fillets
1 tablespoon peanut oil
1 cup (8 fl oz/225 ml) coconut milk
1 teaspoon palm sugar or brown sugar
1 tablespoon lemon juice
4 spring onions (scallions), sliced

PASTE

2 garlic cloves, chopped
2 teaspoons root ginger, chopped
1 stalk lemongrass, sliced
2 medium chillies, deseeded and sliced
2 candle nuts
1 teaspoon shrimp paste (terasi)
1 teaspoon ground coriander
2 teaspoons peanut oil

Grind or pound the paste ingredients in a mortar with a pestle, or use a food processor. Brush the paste over the fish fillets.

Heat the peanut oil in a large frying pan. Add the fish fillets and cook for 1–2 minutes on each side. Add the coconut milk, sugar and lemon juice and simmer for 2–3 minutes. Serve the fish topped with spring onions.

Shrimp in Hot Sauce (Sambal Udang)

Serves 4

1 lb 2 oz (500 g) raw shrimp (prawns)
20 cluster beans, approximately 5 pods (available from Indian stores)
2 cups (16 fl oz/475 ml) coconut milk
4 potatoes, peeled and cut into wedges
1 tablespoon tamarind juice
1 teaspoon salt

PASTE
5 shallots
2 garlic cloves
5 red chillies, sliced
1/2 teaspoon shrimp paste (terasi)
2 tablespoons oil

Peel the shrimp and remove the intestinal tract. Open the bean pods and remove the beans.

Prepare the paste by grinding or pounding all the paste ingredients except for the oil. Heat the oil and sauté the spice paste until fragrant.

Add the shrimp and sauté until they change colour, a few minutes. Add the beans and coconut milk and bring to the boil, stirring. Add the potatoes and tamarind juice and simmer, uncovered, until the potatoes and shrimp are cooked and sauce has thickened. Season with salt and serve.

GRILLED FISH WITH TOMATO SAMBAL (IKAN BAKAR COLO-COLO)

Serves 4

1 whole fish, approximately 1¾ lb (1 kg), cleaned
1/2 teaspoon salt
1 tablespoon lime juice
2 tablespoons oil
Large piece of banana leaf or aluminium foil, to wrap thefish

COLO-COLO SAMBAL
3 tablespoons lime or lemon juice
2 tomatoes, cut in half and sliced
5 red chillies, seeded and sliced
4 shallots, peeled and sliced
4 tablespoons light soy sauce
4 sprigs basil, chopped

Season the fish with the salt and lime juice, then brush with oil. Wrap the fish in the banana leaf and place the parcel directly on the charcoal of a barbecue or under a grill (broiler). Cook until the fish is cooked.

To make the colo-colo sambal, combine all the ingredients in a bowl and mix well.

The sambal can be poured over the fish when serving or, as is usually the case in Indonesia, put into individual sauce bowls for each diner to add to the fish.

Fish in Banana Leaves (Ikan Panggang)

Serves 4

8 pieces banana leaf or kitchen foil
1 lb 9 oz (750 g) boneless white fish fillets, diced
2 shallots, chopped
2 garlic cloves, chopped
1 tablespoon root ginger, chopped
1/4 teaspoon ground turmeric
2 teaspoons ground coriander
1/3 cup (2½ fl oz/75 ml) coconut milk
Juice of 1 lime
Salt, to taste
4 medium red chillies, deseeded and sliced
4 lime leaves, shredded
Lime wedges, to serve

Prepare the banana leaves by cutting into 15 cm (6 in) square pieces. Dip each leaf in a bowl of bowling water.

Combine the fish, shallots, garlic, ginger, turmeric, coriander, coconut milk, lime juice and salt in a food processor. Process until the mixture comes together.

Divide the mixture evenly into 8 and place in the middle of each banana leaf. Top with chilli and lime leaves. Fold banana leaf over fish, flatten a little and secure ends with cocktail sticks.

Cook the fish on a barbecue for 3 minutes on each side, or cook in a steamer for 3–4 minutes. Serve with wedges of lime.

Seafood Curry
(Kari Ikan Udang Cumi-Cumi)

Serves 4

1 tablespoon peanut oil
1/2 teaspoon ground turmeric
1 teaspoon ground coriander
1 cup (8 fl oz/250 ml) coconut milk
1/4 cup (2 fl oz/60 ml) water
2 tablespoons lime juice
2 teaspoons palm sugar or brown sugar
2 lime leaves, shredded
14 oz (400 g) ling fillets, diced
7 oz (200 g) green shrimp (prawns), heads
   removed and shelled
7 oz (200 g) squid rings
Noodles or rice, to serve

PASTE

2 shallots, chopped
2 garlic cloves, chopped
2 teaspoons root ginger, chopped
3 medium chillies, deseeded and sliced
1 lemongrass stalk, sliced
1/2 teaspoon salt

Grind or pound the paste ingredients in a mortar with a pestle or use a food processor.

Heat the oil in a wok or large frying pan. Add the paste and cook for 1–2 minutes. Add the turmeric and coriander and cook until aromatic. Add the coconut milk, water, lime juice, palm sugar and lime leaves. Bring to the boil, add the seafood and cook for 3–4 minutes, or until the seafood is tender. Serve the seafood with noodles or rice.

Marinated Barbecue Seafood (Udang Cumi-Cumi Bakar)

Serves 4

Bamboo skewers, soaked in water for 15 minutes
1/4 cup (2 fl oz/60 ml) peanut oil
Zest of 2 limes, grated
1/3 cup (2½ fl oz/75 ml) lime juice
3 medium chillies, deseeded and finely chopped
3 garlic cloves, crushed
14 oz (400 g) squid, cut into pieces
16 large green shrimp (prawns), shells removed
1 lb 2 oz (500 g) baby octopus, cleaned and trimmed
Boiled rice, to serve

Combine the oil, lime zest and juice, chillies and garlic in a shallow dish. Score the inside skin of the squid diagonally in both directions.

Thread the shrimp lengthways onto bamboo skewers and brush the marinade over them. Add the squid pieces and octopus and brush with marinade. Leave to marinate in a refrigerator for 30 minutes.

Cook the skewers on a barbecue plate, or chargrill for 5–10 minutes, or until cooked. Serve with side bowls of boiled rice.

SAMBAL FRIED SNAPPER (SAMBAL IKAN GORENG)

Serves 4

1 teaspoon ground cumin
1 teaspoon ground coriander
Zest of 1 lime, grated (shredded)
2 tablespoons lime juice
Salt, to taste
4 small snapper
1/3 cup (1¼ oz) plain (all-purpose) flour
Peanut oil, for cooking

MARINADE
2 shallots, chopped
2 garlic cloves, chopped
2 teaspoons root ginger, chopped
2 medium chillies, deseeded and sliced

Grind or pound the marinade ingredients in a mortar with a pestle, or use a food processor. Add the cumin, coriander, zest and lime juice and salt to the marinade.

Make two slits on each side of the snapper. Brush the mixture over the fish and marinate for 1 hour in the refrigerator. Dip the fish in the flour.

Heat the oil in a wok or large frying pan. Fry the fish for 2–3 minutes on each side, or until crisp on the outside and cooked through. Serve with the sambals (sauces) of your choice.

Noodles and Rice

Noodles and Rice
Two Reliable Staples

Rice, an economic food, and one that can be harvested locally is the traditional focus of every meal in Indonesia.

The Indonesians are masters of making rice interesting, even if it is only accompanied by a small amount of vegetables, fish or meat and/or sambals. The rice absorbs the palate-testing sauces, which makes the dish exciting. Indonesian rice is dry; it is not as sticky as other Asian rice. The exception is glutinous rice, which is usually reserved
for desserts.

The best method of cooking rice is by the absorption method or steaming, as more flavour is thus retained than when boiled. When rice is cooked in coconut milk it takes on a new flavour altogether. Left-over rice can be fried to produce nasi goreng, which must be the world's greatest national dish to be based on left-overs. Nasi goreng bears little similarity to the Chinese version of fried rice.

Yellow rice and coconut rice, a feature of Balinese and Javanese cooking, are celebratory dishes at festivals or special family occasions. Nasi kuning (yellow rice) is a simple and sustaining dish and is the basis of risjtafel.

Noodles are also popular in Indonesia but are not generally eaten in conjunction with rice.

Fried Noodles (Bakmi Goreng)

Serves 4

7 oz (200 g) dried egg noodles or thin noodles
1 tablespoon peanut oil
4 shallots, sliced
1 lb 2 oz (500 g) chicken thigh fillets, diced
2 garlic cloves, crushed
1 carrot, peeled and finely sliced or grated (shredded)
2 cups (8 oz/225 g) Chinese cabbage, shredded
2 tablespoons sweet soy sauce (kecap manis)
$1/3$ cup (2½ fl oz/75 ml) chicken stock
1 cup (4 oz/115 g) beansprouts
4 spring onions (scallions), sliced

Cook the noodles following the packet directions. Drain and set aside.

Heat the oil in a wok. Add the shallots and cook until golden. Add the chicken and garlic and stir-fry until just cooked. Add carrots and stir-fry for another 2 minutes. Add the cabbage, kecap manis and stock and continue to cook until the cabbage is wilted.

Add the noodles, beansprouts and spring onions and stir-fry until heated through.

Fried Rice (Nasi Goreng)

2 cups (14 oz/400 g) long-grain rice, rinsed

1 1/2 tablespoons peanut oil

2 eggs, lightly beaten

4 green shallots, finely sliced

2 garlic cloves, crushed

2 small red chillies, deseeded and finely chopped

11 oz (300 g) chicken thigh fillets, diced

1 carrot, finely sliced or grated

2 cups (8 oz/225 g) shredded Chinese cabbage

3 1/2 oz (100 g) shrimp (prawns), peeled and cooked

2–3 tablespoons sweet soy sauce (kecap manis)

1 tablespoon soy sauce

Cook the rice in boiling salted water for 10–12 minutes, or until cooked. Drain and rinse.

Heat 2 teaspoons of the oil in a wok. Add the egg and swirl to coat the wok to form an omelette. Flip the omelette and cook the other side. Remove and cut into thin strips.

Heat the remaining oil in wok. Add the green shallots, garlic and chilli and cook for 1–2 minutes. Add the chicken and stir-fry for 3 minutes. Add the carrot, cabbage, shrimp, kecap manis and soy sauce and stir-fry until the cabbage wilts.

Add the rice to the mixture and stir-fry until heated through. Serve rice with strips of omelette, fried shallots and the sambal (sauce) of your choice.

This dish can be served as a meal with chicken satay and garnished with a fried egg.
Ingredients in rice can vary to suit your taste. If serving with meats you can omit the chicken and shrimp.

Yellow Rice (Nasi Kuning)

1 tablespoon vegetable oil
1 teaspoon ground turmeric
1 teaspoon ground coriander
$1/2$ teaspoon ground cumin
2 cups (14 oz/400 g) long-grain rice, rinsed
2 cups (16 fl oz/500 ml) coconut milk
1 cup (8 fl oz/250 ml) water
6–8 curry leaves
1 cinnamon stick

Heat the oil in a large saucepan. Add the turmeric, coriander, cumin and rice. Stir for 1 minute to coat the rice and cook until aromatic.

Add the coconut milk, water, curry leaves and cinnamon stick and bring to the boil. Reduce the heat to low and cook for 10–12 minutes or until the liquid is absorbed. Transfer the rice to a steamer and steam the rice for 12–15 minutes, stirring from time to time, or until the grains are light. If you don't have a steamer, continue to cook the rice on the lowest heat for 5–10 minutes, or until cooked. Remove the curry leaves and cinnamon stick and serve immediately.

This rice is traditionally served at special occasions.

Fragrant Rice (Nasi Gurih)

1 tablespoon vegetable oil
2 garlic cloves, crushed
6 spring onions (scallions), sliced
1 teaspoon ground coriander
$1/2$ teaspoon galangal powder
2 cups (14 oz/400 g) long-grain rice, rinsed
2 cups (16 fl oz/500 ml) coconut milk
$1/2$–1 cup (4–8 fl oz/125–250 ml) water
6–8 curry leaves

Heat the oil in a large saucepan. Add the garlic, spring onions, coriander, galangal powder and rice. Stir for 1 minute to coat the rice and cook until aromatic.

Add the coconut milk, water and curry leaves and bring to the boil. Reduce the heat to low and cook for 10 minutes, stirring from time to time, or until the liquid is absorbed. Transfer the rice to a steamer and steam for 10–12 minutes, or until the grains are light. If you don't have a steamer continue to cook the rice at the lowest heat for 5–10 minutes, or until cooked. Remove the curry leaves and serve immediately.

CHICKEN RICE WITH PINEAPPLE (NASI KEBULI)

2 tablespoons butter or oil

1 lb 2 oz (500 g) boneless chicken, diced
  into $^3/_8$ in (1 cm) cubes

3 cups (24 fl oz/750 ml) chicken stock

1 teaspoon salt

2 cups (14 oz/400 g) long-grain rice,
  washed and drained

$^1/_2$ small pineapple, peeled and sliced
  then cut into small pieces, to serve

Fried shallot, to serve

SEASONING

13 shallots, peeled and finely chopped

7 garlic cloves, peeled and finely chopped

1 in (2.5 cm) piece of root ginger, peeled
  and chopped

1 teaspoon coriander

$^1/_2$ teaspoon white peppercorns

$^1/_2$ teaspoon cumin

Nutmeg, freshly grated

3 in (8 cm) cinnamon stick (quill)

4 cardamom pods, bruised

2 cloves

1 lemongrass stalk, bruised

Heat the butter or oil in a wok or heavy saucepan. Add all the seasoning ingredients and sauté for 2–3 minutes. Add the chicken and continue sautéing for 3 minutes over high heat.

Add the chicken stock and salt and simmer until the chicken is tender. Strain the stock and put chicken pieces aside.

Put the rice in a rice cooker or heavy stock pot, add 2$^1/_2$ cups (18 fl oz/550 ml) of the reserved chicken stock and bring to the boil. Cover the pan and simmer until the rice is almost cooked and the liquid is absorbed. Add the diced chicken and cook over low heat until the rice is thoroughly cooked.

Serve on a platter garnished with fried shallots and pineapple pieces.

Corn Rice (Nasi Jagung)

Serves 4

1¹/2 cups (11 oz/300 g) rice, washed thoroughly
1¹/2 cups (9 oz/250 g) sweet corn kernels cut from
  raw corn cobs, or canned corn

Put the rice and corn kernels in a pan with 3 cups (24 fl oz/750 ml) of water and bring to the boil. If using canned corn, do not add at this stage.

Simmer the rice and corn until the water is absorbed. If using canned sweetcorn, add it now. Reduce the heat to low and cook the rice and corn for another 10 minutes, until the rice is dry and fluffy. Serve immediately.

White Rice (Nasi Putih)

Serves 4

2 cups (14 oz/400 g) short-grain rice
2–3 cups (16–24 fl oz/500–750 ml) water
1 teaspoon salt

Combine the rice, water and salt in a large saucepan. Bring to the boil. Reduce the heat to very low, cover and allow to steam for 15 minutes, or until the rice is tender before serving.

Vegetables and Noodles in Curry (Kari Sayur)

Serves 4

2 teaspoons peanut oil

$1/2$ teaspoon ground turmeric

1 teaspoon ground cumin

$1/2$ cup (4 fl oz/125 ml) coconut milk

1 cup (8 fl oz/250 ml) chicken stock

2 teaspoons brown sugar

1 head broccoli, cut into florets

$1/2$ cauliflower, cut into florets

1 carrot, sliced

1 lb 6 oz (600 g) fresh thin noodles

PASTE

1 garlic clove, chopped

1 shallot, chopped

1 medium chilli, deseeded and chopped

2 teaspoons peanut oil

Crush or pound the paste ingredients in a mortar with a pestle, or use a food processor.

Heat the remaining oil in a saucepan. Add the paste and stir-fry for 1–2 minutes. Add the turmeric and cumin and stir-fry until aromatic. Add the coconut milk, chicken stock, brown sugar, broccoli, cauliflower and carrot. Bring to the boil, then reduce the heat. Cover and cook for 6–8 minutes, or until the vegetables are tender. Stir in the noodles and serve.

Vegetables

Vegetables
Rich from the soil

In Bali and almost everywhere else in Indonesia, particularly in rural areas, fresh, steamed vegetables are available from roadside stalls as well as in restaurants and hotels. Vegetables are very much a part of meals in Indonesia. No rijstafel would be authentic without vegetables. Indonesia also has an exclusive specialty; fermented soybean cake tempeh.

The island nation has its own indigenous vegetables, which thrive in rich volcanic soil. The vegetable selection was broadened by European conquerors such as the Dutch who discovered that tomatoes, beans, cabbages and carrots would grow well in Indonesia. Much earlier, the Chinese had planted eggplant (aubergine), cucumbers and spinach, which also thrived. Sweet corn kernels, beansprouts and cauliflower are also grown. The Indonesians frequently combine vegetables and fruit and, in addition, vegetables with tofu.

Gado gado is a national dish, which includes eggs, potatoes and peanut sauce. It is time-consuming to prepare but it is a healthy and delicious dish, especially if tofu is added.

Indonesian-style vegetables can be stir-fried, fried, stuffed into pancakes, simmered in coconut milk, made into croquettes and fritters or used to give a spicy flavour to omelettes. Along with rice, at least two vegetable dishes should be served in a traditional Indonesian meal. For example, add corn, peanuts, cumin, garlic, ginger and spring onions (scallions) to your basic pancake or fritter recipe and serve them either as an entrée or as an accompaniment to a main meal.

GREEN BEANS WITH SOY SAUCE (BUNCIS KECAP)

Serves 4

1 tablespoon peanut oil
1 teaspoon sesame oil
1 garlic clove, crushed
2 shallots, sliced
11 oz (300 g) green (French) beans, trimmed and halved
2 tablespoons soy sauce
2 tablespoons water
1 cup (4 oz/115 g) beansprouts, trimmed
1/3 cup (1¼ oz/40 g) roasted peanuts, chopped

Heat the oil in a wok or frying pan. Add the sesame oil, garlic, shallots and beans. Stir-fry for 2–3 minutes. Add the soy sauce and water and cook for 3–4 minutes, or until the beans are just cooked. Stir through the beansprouts and peanuts. Serve warm or cold.

Vegetables with Peanut Sauce (Gado Gado)

Serves 4

2 large potatoes, peeled and cooked
5 oz (150 g) snake beans (Chinese long beans), blanched
2 carrots, sliced and blanched
3½ oz (100 g) beancurd, diced and deep fried
4 eggs, hard-boiled and quartered
1 cucumber, sliced
1 cup (4 oz/115 g) beansprouts, trimmed
Peanut sauce (see recipe)
Sambals (sauces) of your choice, to serve

Place vegetables on a large platter and serve with peanut sauce and the sambals of your choice.

Vegetables in Coconut Milk (Sayur Lodeh)

1 tablespoon peanut oil

1 onion, sliced

2 garlic cloves, crushed

1 teaspoon shrimp paste (terasi), crushed

2 candle nuts, crushed

1 cup (8 fl oz/250 ml) coconut milk

1 cup (8 fl oz/250 ml) chicken stock

1 teaspoon sambal ulek

1 stalk lemongrass, bruised

1 piece broccoli, cut into florets

1/4 cauliflower, cut into florets

1 large zucchini (courgette), halved and sliced

5 oz (150 g) green (French) beans, sliced

Heat the oil in a large saucepan. Add the onion and cook for 2–3 minutes, or until soft. Add the garlic, terasi and candle nuts and cook for 1 minute.

Add the coconut milk, chicken stock, sambal ulek and lemongrass. Bring to the boil. Add the broccoli and cauliflower and simmer, covered, for 4 minutes. Add the zucchini and beans and continue to cook for 3–4 minutes, or until the vegetables are just tender.

Remove the lemongrass and serve.

Spicy Snake Beans (Sambal Buncis)

Serves 4

2 teaspoons peanut oil
1/2 cup (4 fl oz/25 ml) chicken stock
1 stalk lemongrass, bruised
9 oz (250 g) snake beans (Chinese long beans), trimmed

PASTE
2 medium red chillies, deseeded and sliced
2 shallots, chopped
2 teaspoons root ginger, chopped
2 teaspoons garlic, chopped
Vegetable oil (optional)

Grind or pound the paste ingredients in a mortar with a pestle, or use a small food processor. If using a food processor you may need to add a little oil.

Heat the peanut oil in a wok or frying pan. Add the paste and cook for 1–2 minutes. Add the stock and lemongrass. Bring to the boil. Add the beans and cook for 8–10 minutes, or until the beans are tender.

Asian greens can be used instead of beans.

Spicy Fried Eggplant (Terung Goreng)

Serves 4

1/2 cup (4 fl oz/125 ml) peanut oil

2 eggplant (aubergines), cut into 3/8 in (1 cm) slices

2 onions, sliced

2 garlic cloves, crushed

2 small chillies, deseeded and finely chopped

1 teaspoon ground coriander

2 tablespoons tamarind concentrate

1/4 cup (2 fl oz/55 ml) water

1 teaspoon palm sugar or brown sugar

2 spring onions (scallions), sliced

Reserving 1 tablespoon of oil, brush the eggplant slices with some of the remainder.

Heat a large non-stick frying pan. Add the eggplants and cook for 1–2 minutes on each side until golden. Remove and set aside.

Heat the remaining oil. Add the onions and cook for 4–5 minutes, or until golden. Add the garlic, chillies, coriander, tamarind, water and sugar. Return the eggplant to the pan and cook until the sauce reduces. Garnish with spring onions. Serve with side bowls of boiled rice.

Sour Vegetables
(Sayur Asam)

Serves 4

1 tablespoon peanut oil
1 teaspoon galangal powder
1 cup (8 fl oz/250 ml) chicken stock
2 tablespoons tamarind concentrate
1 teaspoon palm sugar or brown sugar
2 zucchinis (courgettes), sliced
1 eggplant (aubergine), diced, or 3 baby eggplants (aubergines), sliced
1 cup (4 oz/115 g) shredded cabbage
5 oz (150 g) green (French) beans

PASTE
2 shallots, chopped
2 garlic cloves
2 medium chillies, deseeded and chopped
1 teaspoon shrimp paste (terasi)
Vegetable oil (optional)

Crush or pound the paste ingredients in a mortar with a pestle or use a small food processor. If using a food processor you may need to add a little oil.

Heat the peanut oil in a wok or saucepan. Add the paste and galangal powder and cook for 1 minute. Add the chicken stock, tamarind and sugar. Bring to the boil, add the vegetables and cook for 6–8 minutes or until the vegetables are tender. Serve as a main or side dish.

Fried Beancurd in Soy Sauce (Tahu Goreng Kecap)

Serves 4

1/2 cup (4 fl oz/125 ml) peanut oil
9 oz (250 g) beancurd, diced
2 teaspoons peanut oil, extra
2 teaspoons root ginger, grated (crushed)
2 medium chillies, deseeded and sliced
1/4 cup (4 fl oz/125 ml) soy sauce
2 tablespoons water
2 teaspoons palm sugar or brown sugar
7 oz (200 g) snow peas (mange tout), trimmed and halved
1 cup (4 oz/115 g) beansprouts, trimmed

Heat the oil in a wok or frying pan. Add the beancurd and cook until golden and crisp. Remove and set aside.

Heat the extra oil and add the ginger and chillies. Stir-fry for 1–2 minutes. Add the soy sauce, water, sugar, beancurd and snow peas. Stir-fry for 2–3 minutes or until tender. Stir the beansprouts through and serve.

SPICY FRIED TEMPEH (SAMBAL GORENG TEMPE)

Serves 4

1/2 cup (4 fl oz/125 ml) peanut oil
11 oz (300 g) tempeh, cut into thin strips
2 teaspoons peanut oil, extra
2 cloves garlic, crushed
1/2 teaspoon shrimp paste (terasi)
1 tablespoon tamarind concentrate
2 tablespoon soy sauce
1 teaspoon palm sugar or brown sugar
2 tablespoons water
2 spring onions (scallions), sliced
1 medium red chilli, deseeded and sliced

Heat the peanut oil in a wok or frying pan. Cook the tempeh in batches until golden and crisp. Remove and set aside.

Heat the extra oil, garlic and shrimp paste and cook for 30 seconds. Add the tamarind, soy sauce, sugar, water and tempeh. Cook until the sauce has reduced.

Garnish with sliced spring onions and chillies. Serve as a main or side dish.

Mixed Vegetable Salad (Jukut Urab)

1/4 Chinese cabbage, shredded
5 oz (150 g) snake beans (Chinese long beans), blanched and sliced
1 bunch spinach, shredded
1 cup (4 oz/115 g) beansprouts, trimmed
1–2 long red chillies, deseeded and sliced
2 tablespoons shredded coconut, toasted
1/4 cup (1 oz/30 g) peanuts, toasted

DRESSING
1/4 cup (2 fl oz/60 ml) vegetable oil
2 tablespoons lime juice
1 tablespoon white vinegar
1 teaspoon sambal ulek
1 teaspoon brown sugar

Combine the cabbage, snake beans, spinach, beansprouts, chillies, coconut and peanuts in a large serving dish.

Combine the oil, lime juice, vinegar, sambal ulek and sugar in a jug (pitcher). Pour dressing over the salad and toss to combine. Serve as a main or side dish.

Desserts

Desserts

With such a plethora of delectable tropical fruits, it's natural that Indonesians serve their fruits peeled and served either whole or sliced. They also use fruit as additions to other desserts, such as blancmange with lychees and pineapple. Banana balls are regarded as a national dish in Indonesia. Other desserts made from glutinous or sticky rice, when combined with coconut milk and palm sugar syrup, satisfy the many Indonesians who have a sweet tooth.

In Sumatra and Java, steamed coconut pudding is a simple favourite, while rice cake, loved also in Sumatra, and Balinese sticky rice dumplings, appeal to most Western tastes. Pancakes are a hit when made with shredded coconut and coconut milk. These pancakes puff up with the addition of ground unsalted peanuts, sesame seeds and baking powder. You can't go wrong with banana or pineapple fritters if presenting a dinner party on any tropical Asian theme. In Indonesia, fritter batter is made from tapioca flour, coconut milk and shredded coconut with baking powder and salt. Pancakes or crêpes prepared with brown rice and plain flour, stuffed with mangoes and drizzled with coconut cream and sugar syrup are sensational.

Can you imagine a fruit salad of chopped grapefruit, orange, green apples, lemon juice and pineapple mixed with diced cucumber, dried shrimp paste, sambal ulek (traditional chilli sauce), soy sauce and sugar? Grilled (broiled) for a few minutes in foil, it will awaken any drowsy dinner guest with a jolt. Cakes are also baked for important celebrations.

However, as in other parts of Asia, these desserts are not often served to finish a meal but as festive food to be taken with Chinese tea and on special occasions. In addition to the fruits named above, Indonesian fresh fruit desserts include jackfruit, tangerines, papayas, rambutans, avocados, breadfruit, lychees, tangerines and mangosteens. Indonesia is reputed to grow more than 40 different types of banana.

Fruit Salad in Spicy Lime Syrup (Rujak)

Serves 4

1/2 pineapple, diced
1 mango, diced
1 papaya, diced
1 apple, cored and diced
1 cucumber, diced
12 rambutans, peeled and deseeded

SYRUP
1 cup (6 oz/175 g) grated palm sugar or brown sugar
1/3 cup (2½ fl oz/75 ml) water
Zest of 1 lime
2 tablespoons lime juice
1 teaspoon tamarind concentrate
1 medium chilli, deseeded and finely chopped

Combine the sugar, water, zest and lime juice in a small saucepan to make the syrup. Bring to the boil and simmer over low heat for 8–10 minutes and allow to cool. Add the tamarind and chilli and stir to combine.

Combine the fruit in a serving bowl. Pour over the syrup and toss before serving.

Coconut Pancakes (Dadar Gulang)

Makes 8

1/2 cup (2 oz/55 g) plain (all-purpose) flour
1 tablespoon caster (superfine) sugar
2 eggs, lightly beaten
3/4 cup (6 fl oz/175 ml) milk or coconut milk
Oil spray, for cooking
1 cup (6 oz/175 g) grated palm sugar or brown sugar
1/2 cup (4 fl oz/125 ml) water
1 pandan leaf
1 cup (4 oz/115 g) shredded coconut, toasted
1 papaya, diced
Ice cream, to serve

Combine the flour and sugar in a mixing bowl. Add the eggs and milk and whisk until the mixture is smooth. Add a little water if it is too thick.

Heat a frying pan. Spray with oil, then add enough mixture to make a thin pancake. Cook the pancakes for 1–2 minutes on each side.

Combine the palm sugar, water and pandan leaf in a saucepan. Bring to the boil and simmer over low heat, stirring until the sugar dissolves and the syrup thickens slightly.

Place the coconut and papaya on each pancake and roll up. Serve the pancakes with ice cream and drizzle with syrup.

Fried Banana (Pisang Goreng)

3/4 cup (5 oz/150 g) rice flour
1 teaspoon ground cinnamon
1 teaspoon caster (superfine) sugar
2/3 cup (5 fl oz/150 ml) water
3 bananas, peeled
Vegetable oil, for cooking
Cream or ice cream, to serve

Combine the flour, cinnamon, sugar and water in a mixing bowl. Whisk the mixture together until it makes a smooth batter.

Cut the bananas in half lengthways and then into pieces. Dip the pieces in the batter.

Heat the oil in a wok or frying pan, add the coated banana pieces and cook until golden and crisp. Serve with cream or ice cream.

Fried Banana Cakes (Pisang Goreng)

6 medium ripe bananas, peeled
1 tablespoon white (granulated) sugar
1 tablespoon plain (all-purpose) flour
Oil, for deep-frying

Mash the bananas and mix with the sugar and sifted flour. Heat the oil in a wok and drop in a large spoonful of batter. Cook several at a time, but do not overcrowd the wok or the temperature of the oil will be lowered. When the cakes are crisp and golden brown, drain on kitchen paper. Serve warm.

Fruit in Coconut Milk (Es Kolak)

Serves 4

4 cups (1¾ pints 1 litre) coconut milk
4 tablespoons palm sugar syrup
Pinch of salt
1 large or 2 small bananas, sliced
2 pieces of ripe jackfruit, finely diced
1 small sweet potato, peeled, diced,
   and simmered until soft

Combine the coconut milk, palm sugar and salt in a pitcher then add all the remaining ingredients. Add a few ice cubes and serve.

Avocado Shake (Es Apokat)

Serves 4

4 ripe avocados, halved and flesh removed
$1/2$ cup ($2^1/2$ oz/75 g) palm sugar syrup (see recipe)
4 tablespoons condensed milk
1 tablespoon lime juice
3 cups ice cubes

Combine the avocado flesh with all other the ingredients and purée in a blender until smooth. Serve in 4 hi-ball glasses.

Black Rice Pudding (Bubur Injin)

Serves 4–6

1¹/2 cups (300 g/11 oz) black glutinous rice
4–4¹/2 cups (1¾ pints/1 litre) water
1 pandan leaf
¹/2 cup (2¹/2 oz/75 g) palm sugar syrup (see below)
Coconut milk or ice cream to serve

PALM SUGAR SYRUP

1 cup (5 oz/150 g) grated palm sugar or brown sugar
¹/2 cup (4 fl oz/125 ml) water

Rinse the rice under cold running water for 1–2 minutes, or until the water is clear.

Combine the rice, water and pandan leaf in a large saucepan. Bring to the boil and simmer over low heat for 40 minutes. Add the syrup and cook for another 10 minutes, or until the rice is tender and the liquid has been absorbed.

To make the syrup, combine the sugar and water in a small saucepan. Bring to the boil and simmer for 8–10 minutes.

Serve with coconut milk or ice cream.

Banana and Coconut Cake (Kue Pisang Dan Kelapa)

Serves 6–8

4 $1/2$ oz (125 g) butter, at room temperature
1 cup (7 oz/200 g) caster (superfine) sugar
2 eggs
3 ripe bananas
$1/2$ cup (4 fl oz/125 ml) lemon juice
$11/2$ cups (6 oz/175 g) self-raising (self-rising) flour
$1/2$ teaspoon bicarbonate soda (baking soda)
$1/2$ teaspoon ground cinnamon
1 cup (4 oz/115 g) desiccated (dry unsweetened shredded) coconut
Cream, ice cream or fruit, to serve

Preheat the oven to 180°C/350°F/Gas mark 4. Lightly grease an 8 in (20 cm) cake tin (pan) and line the base with baking paper.

Cream the butter and sugar in a mixing bow until light and fluffy. Add the eggs, one at a time, and beat well after each addition.

Place bananas in a food processor with the lemon juice. Blend until very mushy. Stir the bananas through the mixture. Add the flour, bicarbonate of soda, cinnamon and coconut. Stir until combined.

Spoon the batter into the prepared cake tin and bake for 40–45 minutes, or until a skewer comes out clean. Leave to set for 10–15 minutes, then turn out onto a cake rack to go cold.

Cut into wedges and serve with cream or ice cream and fruit.

SAMBALS, PASTES AND CONDIMENTS

There are a few pastes and Indonesian instant spice mixes available in Chinese stores. Sambal ulek also called sambal oelek is readily available in supermarkets.

BASIC SPICE PASTE (SAMBAL)

4 shallots, chopped
4–6 small red chillies, deseeded
2 cloves garlic
2 teaspoons fresh ginger, chopped
1 lemongrass stalk, chopped
Peanut oil, (optional)

Grind all the ingredients in a mortar with a pestle or use a food processor. If using a food processor add a little oil to process.

CHILLI SAMBAL (SAMBAL BAJAK)

4 shallots, chopped
4 small red chillies, deseeded and
   chopped
2 garlic cloves, chopped
4 candle nuts

1 teaspoon shrimp paste (terasi)
$1^1/_2$ tablespoons peanut oil
1 tablespoon tamarind concentrate
1 tablespoon palm sugar or brown sugar

Crush or pound the shallots, chillies, garlic, candlenuts and terasi with 2 teaspoons peanut oil in a mortar with pestle or a food processor. Process until smooth. Heat the remaining oil in a frying pan or wok. Add paste and stir-fry for 1–2 minutes. Add the tamarind and sugar. Keep in an airtight container in the refrigerator for 8–10 days.

TOMATO SAMBAL (SAMBAL TOMATO)

Shallots, peeled
4 small red chillies
2 tomatoes
2 tablespoons lime juice

Pinch of salt
2 tablespoons chopped basil leaves

Finely slice the shallots, chillies and tomatoes. Stir in lime juice, salt and chopped basil.

SOY AND CHILLI SAMBAL (SAMBAL KECAP)

2 tablespoons soy sauce
1 tablespoon water
2 tablespoons lemon juice
1 mediumred chilli, deseeded and sliced

1 shallot, sliced
1 garlic clove, crushed

Mix all the ingredients together.

CUCUMBER PICKLES (ACAR SEGAR)

1 tablespoons white vinegar
2¹/₂ tablespoons white sugar
1 teaspoon salt
2¹/₂ tablespoons hot water
1 medium cucumber, peeled, seeded,
    cut lengthwise then sliced

Mix the vinegar, sugar, salt and water until the sugar dissolves, then combine with the cucumber slices and allow to rest for 1 hour before serving.

PICKLED CUCUMBERS AND BEANSPROUTS (DABU-DABU KENARI)

9 oz (250 g) cucumber, peeled and sliced
1 cup (4 oz/115 g) beansprouts, blanched
4 shallots, finely sliced
3 red chillies, sliced
4 sprigs basil
1¾ oz (50 g) kenari nuts or raw almonds,
    peeled and coarsely ground

3 tablespoons lime or lemon juice
¹/₂ teaspoon white (granulated) sugar
¹/₂ teaspoon shrimp paste (terasi), toasted
¹/₂ teaspoon salt

Arrange the cucumber and beansprouts on a plate and scatter with shallots, chillies and basil. Combine the nuts, lime juice, sugar, terasi and salt, adding a little warm water to make a thick sauce. Pour the sauce over the vegetables and serve.

VINEGAR SAMBAL (SAMBAL CUKA)

1/4 cup (1 oz/30 g) roasted peanuts
2 shallots, chopped
3 medium red chillies, deseeded and chopped
2 garlic cloves
2 teaspoons peanut oil
1/4 cup (2 fl oz/60 ml) white vinegar
1 teaspoon palm sugar or brown sugar

Crush or pound the peanuts, shallots, chillies, garlic and oil in a mortar with pestle or a food processor. Mix together with vinegar and sugar.

FRIED SHALLOTS (BAWANG GORENG)

10 shallots, peeled
1/3 cup (2½ fl oz/75 ml) vegetable oil

Thinly slice the shallots. Dry with a kitchen paper.
   Heat the oil in a wok. Add the shallots and fry until golden. Drain on kitchen paper and store in an airtight container.

QUICK PEANUT SAUCE (SAUS KACANG CEPAT)

1/2 cup (2 oz/60 g) crunchy peanut butter
1/2 cup (2 fl oz/60 ml) water
2 teaspoons sambal ulek
1 teaspoon sweet soy sauce (kecap manis)
2 teaspoons lemon juice

Combine the peanut butter and water in a small saucepan. Stir over low heat until the sauce thickens. Remove from the heat and stir in the sambal ulek and kecap manis and allow to cool before adding lemon juice.

SPICED COCONUT WITH PEANUTS (SERUNDENG)

2 teaspoons peanut oil
1/2 teaspoon ground cumin
1 teaspoon ground coriander
1/2 teaspoon galangal powder
1 tablespoon tamarind concentrate
1 cup (4 oz/115 g) shredded coconut
1/2 cup (2 oz/60 g) roasted peanuts

PASTE
1 shallot, chopped
1 garlic clove, chopped
1 teaspoon shrimp paste (terasi)

Crush or pound the ingredients for the paste in a mortar with pestle or process in a food processor.

Heat the oil in a wok or frying pan. Stir-fry the paste for 1–2 minutes. Add the cumin, coriander and galangal, and stir-fry until aromatic. Add the tamarind and coconut and stir-fry over low heat until golden. Stir in the peanuts. Store in an airtight container for 1 week. Serve cold as a garnish. Keeps for about 2 weeks.

PICKLED SHALLOTS
(ACAR BAWANG)

2 tablespoons white vinegar
1 teaspoon salt
1$^1/_2$ tablespoon white sugar
3 tablespoons warm water
24 shallots, peeled and sliced

Mix all the ingredients except for the shallots, stirring until the
sugar dissolves. Combine with the shallots. Leave for 2–3 hours before serving.

PEANUT SAUCE (SAUS KACANG)

$^1/_3$ cup (2½ fl oz/75 ml) peanut oil
3½ oz (100 g) raw peanuts
1 garlic clove
2 shallots
$^1/_2$ teaspoon shrimp paste (terasi)

Salt
2 teaspoons chilli sauce or sambal ulek
$^1/_2$ teaspoon brown sugar
1$^1/_2$–2 cups (12–16 fl oz/375–500 ml) water
Lemon juice, to taste

Heat $^1/_4$ cup (2 fl oz/60 ml) oil in a wok. Add the peanuts and fry for 4–5 minutes, or
until golden. Drain on kitchen paper. When the peanuts are cool, crush in a mortar with
a pestle or process in a food processor.

Crush or pound the garlic, shallots, terasi and salt to a paste.

Heat the remaining oil in a saucepan and cook the paste for 1 minute, or until
aromatic. Add chilli sauce, sugar and water. Bring to the boil, add the peanuts and
simmer for 20–25 minutes, or until the sauce is thick. Add lemon juice to taste.

Glossary

Anchovies, dried (ikan teri): Small salted dried anchovies are used to season some dishes. They are available in most Chinese stores. Unless they are very tiny, anchovies are usually about 1 in (2.5 cm) long. Discard the heads and any black intestinal tract before frying.

Banana leaves: Can be purchased at fruit shops or Chinese supermarkets. They are used for steaming food. The food is usually wrapped in the banana leaf like a parcel. If you cannot buy banana leaves, aluminium foil can be used instead.

Basil (daun selasih, daun kemangi): Two varieties of this fragrant herb are found in Indonesia, generally added to dishes at the last minute for maximum flavour. Daun kemangi has a lemony scent, while daun selasih is more similar to sweet European basil, which can be used as a substitute.

Beancurd (tahu): Is sold in cakes and is compressed to form a hard cake. It is harder than tofu and darker in colour. Beancurd is available in supermarkets and Chinese supermarkets.
Beans (buncis): The common bean available in Indonesia is the snake bean, also called, runner or long bean. Green beans can also be used. Snake beans are available in both supermarkets and fruit shops.

Candle nut (kemiri): This is a round nut like a macadamia nut. Candle nuts are available in Chinese shops. Substitute with macadamia nuts or almonds.

Carambola, sour (belimbing wuluh): This pale green acidic fruit about 2–3 in (5–8 cm) long, grows in clusters on a tree. The fruit, a relative of the large, five-edged sweet star-fruit, carambola is used whole or sliced to give a sour taste to some soups, fish dishes and sambals. Sour grapefruit or tamarind juice can be used as a substitute.
Cardamom (kepulaga): About 8–12 intensely fragrant black, seeds are enclosed in a straw coloured, fibrous pod. Try to buy the whole pod rather than cardamom seeds or powder. For maximum flavour, bruise lightly with the back of a cleaver to break the pod before adding to food.

Cassava (ubi kayu): The root of this plant, and the tender green leaves, are both used as a vegetable. The root is also grated (shredded) and mixed with coconut and sugar to make a number of cakes. Fermented cassava root is added to some dessert dishes, while the dried root is made into small balls (tapioca) and used in the same way as pearl sago. Substitute spinach for cassava leaves.

Celery (seledri): The celery used in Indonesia is different from the Western variety. Indonesian celery has slender stems and particularly pungent leaves and is often referred to as 'Chinese celery' abroad. It is used as a herb rather than a vegetable.

Chilli paste (sambal ulek or oelek): This is a basic chilli paste, made from crushed chillies.

Chillies (cabai, cabe or lombok): Indonesians mostly use small red chillies, which are known as bird's eye chillies. These chillies are very hot. When deseeding and cutting chillies it is best to wear gloves because the juice may burn your skin.

Chives (kucai): Coarse chives, with flat leaves about 12 in (30 cm) long, are used as a seasoning. Although the flavour of the chive is more delicate, spring onions (scallions) can be used as a substitute.

Cinnamon (kayu manis): The thick, dark brown bark of a type of cassia is used in Indonesia. It is not true cinnamon. The latter is more subtle in flavour and considerably more expensive. Always use cinnamon quills, not ground cinnamon.

Cloves (cengkih): This small, brown, nail-shaped spice was once found only in the islands of Maluku. Cloves add their characteristic fragrance to the clove-scented cigarettes or kretek throughout Indonesia.

Coconut milk (santan): Indonesians use fresh coconut in cooking, but it is easier to use tinned or powered coconut milk.

Coriander (ketumbar): Both ground coriander and coriander seeds are used in Indonesian cooking. Coriander seeds are small like peppercorns but lighter in colour.

Cumin (jintan): Together with coriander and pepper, this small beige elongated seed is one of the most commonly used spices in Indonesia. Take care not to confuse it with fennel.

Curry Leaves (daun kari): Available fresh in some fruit shops.

Galangal (laos, lengkuas): This is a member of the ginger family. Dried galangal and galangal powder is also available in Chinese supermarkets.

Garlic (bawang putih): Indonesian garlic cloves are usually smaller and less pungent than that found in many Western countries. Adjust the amount to suit your taste.

Kecap Manis: This is a thick sweet soy sauce. Available in supermarkets and Chinese supermarkets.

Kenari nuts: The canari nut is quite oily and comes from Maluku – substitute with almond.

Lemongrass (serai, sereh): Available in supermarkets and fruit shops. To prepare, slice the white bottom part and crush into a paste. Bruise the top half and tie it in a loose knot. Add the top half to a curry for flavour.

Lime (jeruk nipis): Several types of lime are used in Indonesia. The most fragrant is the leprous or kaffir lime (jeruk purut). It has virtually no juice but the double leaf is often used whole or very finely shredded, while the grated (shredded) skin is occasionally used in cooking. Round yellow-skinned limes, slightly larger than a golf ball, and small, dark green limes are used for their juice. If limes are not available, use lemons.

Palm sugar (gula merah, gula Jawa): Comes in a hard round block. It is available in supermarkets. Substitute with brown sugar.

Pandan leaf (daun pandan): This is a fragrant leaf and is used to flavour desserts and curries. It is usually tied in a knot. Available in some fruit shops.

Peanuts (kacang tanah): These are ground (either raw or cooked) and used to make sauces. Deep-fried peanuts are a very common garnish or condiment. Do not salt fried peanuts before cooling then storing them or they will become soggy.

Salam leaf (daun salam): A subtly flavoured leaf of a member of the cassia family. The flavour bears no resemblance whatsoever to that of bay leaves, which are sometimes suggested as a substitute.

Salted soya beans (tauco): Salty and with a distinctive tang, this Chinese ingredient is used to season some dishes and to make a savoury side-dish or sambal.

Sambal ulek: Indonesian salty chilli paste available in stores.

Shallots (bawang merah): A relative of the onion family, which has small bulbs covered in brown, yellow or pink skin.

Shrimp (prawns), dried (ebi): Used to season some dishes, these should be soaked in warm water for 5 minutes before use and any shell discarded. Choose dried shrimp that are bright pink in colour and avoid any that look grey or mouldy.

Soy sauce (kecap manis or kecap asin): Two types of soy sauce are used in Indonesia: thick sweet soy sauce, which is most frequently used as a condiment, usually with added sliced chillies; and the thinner, saltier light soy sauce.

Spring onion (scallion) (daun bawang): Sometimes known as scallions or green shallots, this popular herb is often used as a garnish and to add flavour to many dishes.

Star anise (bunga lawang, pekak): An 8-pointed star-shaped spice, dark brown in colour, with each point containing a shiny brown, round seed. It has a strong aniseed or licorice flavour.

Tamarind (asam jawa): Is used to give a sour taste to a dish. It is available in a block, and needs to be mixed with water. It is easier to use concentrate, which comes in a screw-top jar. Available in Chinese supermarkets.

Tapioca (telur ubi kayu): see Cassava.

Tempeh (tempe): This is a compressed cake of soya beans. Available in supermarkets and Chinese supermarkets.

Terasi (trasi, blachan, belachan, shrimp paste): This comes in a hard block. When cooking cut off the required amount and add to paste or, to pre-cook terasi, dry-fry a small amount wrapped in foil. Available in Chinese supermarkets.

Turmeric (kunyit): This is a member of the ginger family. Fresh turmeric is available in some fruit shops and Chinese supermarkets. Ground turmeric is readily available.

Yam bean (bangkuang): Used in salads and some cooked vegetable dishes; water chestnuts make an acceptable substitute.

Index

About the Author

Mae Chandra grew up in Indonesia and travelled the world extensively when she finished school. After being asked for cooking lessons and recipes numerous times, Mae wrote *Indonesian* to share her encyclopedic knowledge of food from her home region.